# Airgun Shooting
## ~ An Introduction ~

### Les Herridge

**Peter Andrew Publishing
Company Limited**

Copyright © Les Herridge 1994

All rights reserved

First published in 1994 by

PETER ANDREW PUBLISHING COMPANY LIMITED
4, Charlecot Road, Droitwich, Worcestershire, WR9 7RP

ISBN 0 946796 58 0

A CIP catalogue record for this book is available from the British Library

Typeset in Great Britain by
Peter Andrew Publishing Company Limited

Printed and bound in Great Britain

This book is sold subject to the condition that it shall not, by way of trade or otherwise, be lent, resold, hired out, or otherwise circulated without the publisher's consent, in any form of binding or cover other than in which it is published and without a similar condition including this condition being imposed on the subsequent publisher.

# Contents

|    | | |
|----|---|---|
|    | Introduction ... ... ... ... | ... iv |
|    | Acknowledgements ... ... ... ... | ... iv |
| 1. | Airguns: Law and Safety ... ... ... | ... 1 |
| 2. | Choosing an Airgun ... ... ... ... | ... 11 |
| 3. | Somewhere to Shoot ... ... ... | ... 23 |
| 4. | Using the Gun ... ... ... ... | ... 31 |
| 5. | Understanding Ballistics ... ... ... | ... 40 |
| 6. | Competitive Airgun Shooting ... ... | ... 51 |
| 7. | In Conclusion ... ... ... ... | ... 65 |
|    | Index ... ... ... ... | ... 67 |

# Introduction

My aim in writing this book has been to answer, in as straightforward a manner as possible, those questions which are commonly raised by newcomers to the sport of airgun shooting. I have tried to cover most aspects, from choosing a gun through to competitive shooting and vermin control. I have also outlined the importance of safety and of a mature approach to the sport.

Airgun shooting is a highly enjoyable and relatively inexpensive pastime which is available to a wide age group. It can provide many hours of pleasure and relaxation, and I hope that you will gain as much enjoyment from your shooting as I have done over the years.

Please always remember to act responsibly when you are dealing with guns and so help to maintain the high standards which are being established for this increasingly popular sport.

# Acknowledgements

I would like to thank Ian Law for his valued assistance in the preparation of the sections relating to competitive shooting.

## Chapter 1

# Airguns:
# Law and Safety

Most of us have seen teenagers on a canal towpath or river bank, happily blasting away with an airgun at tin cans in the water, or shooting at bottles on a council rubbish tip. What we may not have realised is that they were almost certainly breaking the law. The chances are that they did not know it either. Shooting is not permitted in any public place, and a public place may be defined as anywhere the public at large has a legal right to be: pavements, roads, public footpaths, public parks, public car parks, canal towpaths (if they are open to the public), seaside promenades and so on.

The law is intended to protect people from possible injury, so the 'no public places' clause is an eminently sensible one. However, it is one which is frequently ignored, sometimes resulting in accidents, which, apart from their own immediate and often serious consequences, can lead to hysterical cries for the banning of all air weapons, or at least for a tightening of the law involving them. We shall see, though, that the law referring to airguns is already very strict indeed. If it were fully understood accidents would be few, and the sport would be less maligned than it tends to be at present. Be in no doubt, airguns are not toys, and even the relatively low powered examples can cause serious injury, even death, if misused. People have been permanently blinded and paralysed by airgun pellets, and accidents can occur very quickly in an unguarded moment. Always regard your airgun as loaded, whether it is or not, and *never* point a gun at anyone, nor at any animal. It is worth remembering that many people have been injured or even killed by 'unloaded' guns.

A pellet, which is propelled by an airgun or pistol at the relatively low velocity of 300 feet per second, will penetrate into softwood from quite a considerable distance. Imagine what it will do to human flesh. Although the maximum power of air rifles and pistols is restricted by law to 12 foot pounds muzzle energy and 6 foot pounds energy respectively, a rifle on the legal limit will project a .22 pellet at more than 600 feet per second, or more than 800 feet per second if the rifle is in .177 calibre. Pistol velocities are, naturally, somewhat less, but still above 300 feet per second.

Domestic animals are sometimes shot at by irresponsible people, but often by a gardener who simply wants to dissuade cats from spoiling his garden. To frighten a cat from his garden, the gardener lets fly with what he believes to be a stinging shot from a low powered air pistol or rifle, and has the satisfaction of seeing the startled animal leap into the air and run away, apparently quite unharmed, but suitably 'warned'. The cat makes its way to a quiet shed where it lies down in a corner and licks at a small hole in its side. A week later, it dies, in the same place, in considerable pain from its wound. The owner, who eventually finds the unfortunate animal, may, understandably, write a vitriolic letter to the local newspaper, decrying the use of airguns. My own pedigree Siamese died in identical circumstances, and my vet informed me that death and injury among domestic pets from airgun misuse is extremely common. If you shoot at any domestic animal you may be breaking more than one law. Cruelty to animals is an obvious offence, but if you are shooting in a public place, that is an additional offence. Shoot across someone else's garden and you still break the law. If you are under age without supervision, yet another offence is committed. Shooting law is very complex, and it is, therefore, very important to understand it clearly to avoid transgression.

## ❑ Age Restrictions

The law is strict regarding young people and airguns. Boys and girls of all ages can be fascinated by airguns, and often progress from cap guns of childhood to the potential danger of airguns. Statistics indicate that young teenagers are responsible for most of the ill-effects which are the result of the use, or misuse, of airguns.

Children under 14 years are forbidden by law to own an airgun at all, and may only use one if they are supervised by an adult

# Airguns: Law and Safety

*Be sure you understand the Law before you start shooting.*

over 21. They are also, like anyone else, prevented from using an airgun in public places. It is worth mentioning that the supervising adult may be held responsible for any misdemeanour committed by the youngster. The principle is not unlike that of a learner driver who needs to be accompanied by an experienced driver, at all times.

Between the ages of 14 and 17 years, youngsters are not legally allowed to buy an airgun or ammunition, but someone over 17, usually their parent, may buy these for them, and then they may shoot unsupervised, provided they are in a place where they have a legal right to be.

Youngsters in this second age group may legally carry an *unloaded* air rifle in a public place, but only if it is in a securely fixed cover and cannot be fired. There are no circumstances where a person under the age of 17 years may have possession

*Airgun Shooting*

of an air pistol (even an unloaded one) in public, except in connection with an approved range or shooting gallery.

## ❏ Trespassing

We have seen that airguns are prohibited from being used in any public place, so it will be apparent that they may only be used on private land or premises, and then only where the shooter has been granted permission to shoot from the owner of the land. Shooting on private land without permission constitutes armed trespass, for which the penalties can be severe. If you are hunting, you may also fall foul of anti-poaching laws and be liable to confiscation of your airgun.

It is worth remembering the simple fact that *all* land is owned by someone. This is a point many people overlook when they see a patch of disused land, or an old abandoned industrial site. The land may not be fenced, and it may be full of rabbits and tempting to a budding hunter, but unless you have permission, preferably in writing, you should not attempt to shoot there. Make an effort to gain the necessary permission beforehand.

Even so-called 'common' land is unsuitable for shooting, since it could technically be regarded as a public place. In areas such as Wales and Scotland, the hills and mountains are often unfenced, and impart the impression that anyone may roam around at will, as indeed walkers and nature lovers often do. But these areas are usually owned by hill farmers, who might well take a dim view of strangers with airguns prowling around among their sheep. The Forestry Commission is another large landowner in Britain, and while its representatives may turn a blind eye to the activities of an airgun enthusiast, it is pointless to take unnecessary chances.

## ❏ Public Awareness

It is important to remember that the general public has an inbuilt fear of any kind of gun. The sight of a stranger, perhaps clad in pseudo-military camouflage clothing, carrying a sinister looking rifle with a telescopic sight on top, and roaming around on land where he has no right to be, could certainly cause alarm. It could also result in the landowner telephoning the local constabulary, and the trespasser may well find himself invited to the police station to help with further enquiries.

In law, to say that you 'did not know' does not constitute a defence. The best that could be hoped for is that your honest face and appropriate pleading might convince the magistrate that your ignorance is genuine, and *may*, therefore, be taken as a mitigating circumstance. That will not stop you from being found guilty, it may simply reduce the sentence. Expect to have your airgun confiscated too.

## ❏ Storing and Transporting an Airgun

The same principle of not alarming the public applies when transporting an airgun. We have looked at what the law says with regard to young people using airguns. The law also makes it clear that people under 17 years of age may only carry an unloaded airgun in public if it is in a securely fastened gun cover to prevent it from being fired, either accidentally or intentionally. Those under 14 years of age may only carry an airgun in public if they are supervised continuously by an adult over the age of 21, and the aforementioned condition, i.e. that the gun be in a securely fastened cover, is, of course, applicable to under-14s.

As I pointed out earlier, the law is eminently sensible so far as it applies to air-powered weapons, and the principle of keeping an airgun in a proper cover is just as sensible as the other requirements. If I were driving my car down a busy road in an urban area and saw several young people carrying uncovered airguns, I should feel a little uneasy myself. Everyone, regardless of age, should keep a gun covered until they are actually in the locality where it is to be used.

## ❏ General Safety and Security

Safety and security go hand in hand so far as any type of gun is concerned, and airguns which are not actually in use should be carefully stored in a secure place. Airguns should not be used or stored within reach of small children. Youngsters are often fascinated with guns, but unfortunately they have little

*Airgun Shooting*

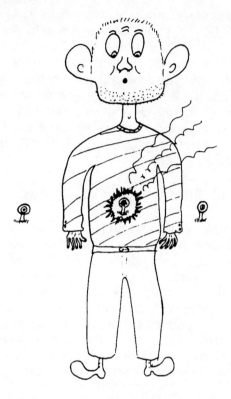

*Safety must always be of paramount importance when shooting.*

real concept of what the dangers are, and regard airguns as mere toys. The results of carelessness can and have led to tragedy.

A securely made gun case with a strong lock is the best means of storing guns away from questing little fingers, and will also help to prevent theft. If your airgun collection is quite valuable, you may like to consider having it insured, but you may find that the insurers will insist upon basic security precautions being taken before they will issue a cover note or policy.

When handling any weapon, even a relatively low powered air pistol, always keep it pointed towards the target area, and keep people, particularly children, away from that area. Avoid waving the gun around, especially while you are loading it, and *never* fool about with it. Never run with a loaded gun either –

that invites trouble. To give yourself a rough idea of the power of your airgun and, hopefully, a sense of healthy respect for it, place a flat sheet of thick steel against a wall, and fire several lead pellets directly and squarely at it from several metres away. You will find that a high powered air rifle will literally shoot the centres out of the pellets, leaving the remnants totally flattened beyond all recognition. Lower powered airguns produce pellets damaged to varying degrees. Admittedly, lead pellets are quite soft and easily deformed, but just imagine what that deformed pellet would have done to your delicate body if it had hit you. So, handle your airgun accordingly, with the respect it merits.

## ❏ Safety with regard to Animals

If you are out hunting, keep away from sheep, cattle, horses and pigs, both when actually shooting and, as far as possible, when stalking. Every year farm animals are hit by airgun pellets, often fired deliberately, but occasionally their injuries are the result of sheer carelessness. Apart from the obvious suffering to the animal, and the veterinary bills which might arise, there is also the possibility that the farmers may become alienated against all airgun users, regardless of who they are, or how they act. Farmers will be less encouraged to allow their land to be used for shooting and are also likely to tell the neighbouring landowners about such cases of misuse of airguns. In this way, more potential shooting land is lost to numerous airgun users.

It really is in the interest of the sport for you to report personally to the police any individuals who are seen shooting at farm animals, asassuming that you do not feel able to put a stop to it yourself. Just remember that if you shut your eyes to the problem, you devalue your own sport. What is more, those involved will continue to misuse their guns until someone else has the strength of mind to stand up for what they know to be right, by which time a great deal of damage may have been done, both to the animals and to the reputation of the sport. These people certainly have nothing in common with serious airgun users, and they comprise an element which must be severely reprimanded if the sport is to survive in its present

## Airgun Shooting

*Treat any gun with respect, and regard it as loaded at all times, whether it is or not.*

form.

Adults have a great part to play in teaching youngsters both about the basic skills of shooting, including safety and careful handling techniques, and the law. The best teacher has always been example, and the attitude of someone who is held in high esteem by a young person will always influence the youngsters far more, for good or bad, than any amount of talking or instruction.

### ❑ Ammunition

Chapter 3 deals with the setting up of an effective backstop for shooting, but it is worth bearing in mind here that some types of airgun ammunition are inclined to bounce about dangerously, unlike the familiar lead pellets, which tend to expend their energy quickly when they hit a hard surface at right angles. BB shots, airgun darts and some nonleaded hunting pellets are the usual culprits. Care should be taken when using these types of ammunition.

Oddly enough, it is often the low powered guns which cause the most dangerous ricochets, as high powered shots usually penetrate or flatten out harmlessly. A shot from a hunting air rifle, for instance, will pierce soft timber at any reasonable range, but a low powered airgun will cause the pellet to bounce off the wood and wend its way back to you – often with painful, or serious, results.

## ❏ Pistols

With pistols, the question of safety should be given even more consideration than with rifles. Due to their compact size and 'pointability', air pistols could possibly be mistaken for toy guns by youngsters. They should, therefore, always be stored well out of reach of children, and, of course, kept unloaded and uncocked. Because of this 'pointability', pistols are inclined to be angled in all directions while being loaded and prepared for firing. Be extremely cautious and guard against accidental discharges, keeping the weapon pointed towards the target area at all times. Insist that anyone shooting with you does the same.

## ❏ Safety Catches

I am not a great believer in safety catches on airguns, because my view is that an airgun should not be loaded and cocked unless it is ready to fire, and that is a far better safety device than any mechanical aid. I will concede, however, that safety catches do have an application in hunting, especially when pump-up guns are used. Pump-ups are noisy to cock, requiring several firm pumps, and it is detrimental to the hunting if this operation needs to be done when the quarry has already been sighted, so a safety catch can be useful here. Safety catches are inclined to make people over-confident, leading to forgetfulness of basic precautions. On balance, therefore, it is my personal opinion that we are better off without them.

# Chapter 2

# Choosing an Airgun

Airguns range in price from a few pounds for a very basic pop-out barrelled pistol to several hundred pounds for a top flight match rifle. Between the two extremes there has grown, in recent years, a vast array of apparently similar weapons, making a beginner's choice difficult. Purchasing on impulse, by appearance only, is like a lucky dip, and will usually lead to disappointment. Parents buying for a youngster will often be confused and unsure about where to go for information.

A good gun dealer will offer free advice and will not put any sort of pressure on a potential customer. Many dealers now have their own range where a customer will often have the opportunity of trying several different weapons.

The first step in choosing an airgun is to determine the type of shooting for which the gun is intended. A powerful hunting rifle would obviously be an unnecessary expense for backyard shooting, apart from being heavy and perhaps a little clumsy in a confined space. Conversely, a low powered pistol or rifle is of little use to a prospective rabbit hunter. Furthermore, a top quality match air rifle is really only suited to competitive target shooting, no matter how attractive it may look in a rack above the mantelpiece.

Another point to remember is that a young person of light build may find a heavy hunting or match rifle very cumbersome to handle. Some powerful air rifles and pistols can be difficult to cock, too, so the golden rule must be 'try it first.'

## ❏ Value for Money

Having decided upon the type of shooting for which the airgun is most likely to be used, the next consideration for many prospective purchasers must be price. Probably the best plan is to list all the airguns which appear to fit your requirements, bearing in mind that there will still be many air weapons which

## Airgun Shooting

*Seek expert advice when choosing an airgun. Many gun dealers have a range where airguns may be tried out.*

fall into the 'general purpose' group, and will, with few exceptions, suit many likely applications. Having listed appropriate guns, those which fall outside your price range can then be eliminated.

The most expensive airguns have traditionally been of German origin. An example is the excellent Weihrauch range, renowned for their fine trigger mechanism and high standard of construction.

In recent years, however, British manufacturers and customisers have realised that there is a steady demand for a product built up to a standard rather than down to a price, and now some of the very best airguns available are of British origin. Names such as Air Arms, Theoben, Titan, Brocock and others have joined the great historic names of Webley and BSA in providing the customer with a greater choice of quality airguns than has ever before been available.

At the lower end of the scale, guns from Spain, Eastern Europe and China can be bought quite cheaply. Airguns from Spain are probably the best of these, and the quality of some Spanish airguns is exceptionally good. Poor finish is often an indication of poor workmanship elsewhere. Some of the first airguns to be imported from China in the late 1970s were cheap but had little else to commend them. There are indications that this situation has since improved, but, if buying secondhand, beware.

Be particularly careful if buying a gun from any of the cheaper, less well-known ranges of airgun, because spares can often be difficult, if not impossible, to find. Fortunately, airguns have few moving parts and are generally reliable, but mainsprings and airseal washers will need replacement eventually, and availability of spares must be a consideration. In practice, a knowledgeable owner or gunsmith can often improvise, using a part adapted from another make of gun, but this is an unnecessary inconvenience.

## ❏ Power

Since the advent of the first airgun magazines in the mid-'seventies and the resurgence of interest in airguns which these magazines have generated, the British airgun industry has undergone something of an upheaval. Some manufacturers have fallen victim to the recession, and have either gone out of business entirely or ceased the manufacture of airguns and concentrated on more viable aspects of their work. Those manufacturers remaining have found it necessary to produce new and better models to cope with the demand for high quality, high powered air rifles, which had previously only been available from the German companies. The competition has, as always, been good for the customer, and buyers are now very much spoilt for choice.

Webley and BSA have a useful range of airguns which have proved consistently popular over the years. Both manufacturers produce air rifles of good quality, with power near the legal limit of 12 foot pounds muzzle energy, as well as retaining the relatively low powered guns intended for youngsters.

Perhaps I could take this opportunity to clarify one particular misconception among beginners to the sport of airgun shooting. Although adequate power is necessary when shooting vermin, to ensure clean, humane kills, it is not always true that the most powerful gun is the best for the job. Consistent accuracy is a far more essential attribute in an airgun, and in fact airguns producing between about 7 and 12 foot pounds energy will cope effectively with small vermin at a sensible range.

Most manufacturers give an idea of the power of the airguns they are selling, and the monthly airgun magazines run regular tests on the most popular guns. It should not, therefore, prove too difficult to establish the relevant details on any gun which might be suitable for your requirements.

## ❏ Calibre

Another question which will need to be considered when buying an airgun is the matter of calibre. A slightly tricky one, this, since even experts disagree as to which calibre is best for a particular application.

The choice, broadly, is between .177 and .22, that is .177 of an inch and .22 of an inch. Some pneumatics are available in .20 calibre, and some older weapons may have other calibres such as .25. However, for most practical purposes, .177 and .22 are the choices when buying an airgun, and it is these which we shall now consider.

The required calibre for serious competitive shooting is .177, and many clubs will insist upon this calibre for that reason. The small pellets have the advantage of travelling at relatively high velocity compared with the heavier .22, giving them a flatter trajectory and a good standard of accuracy. It is also worth remembering that they are less expensive – an important consideration to note, especially if the gun is to be used for plinking, which can be exceptionally heavy on pellets.

The .22 is traditionally the calibre for vermin control with airguns, a tradition which has been fostered by manufacturers over the years. The theory behind their use for vermin control is that they are more forceful than the .177, delivering more shock and thus more killing power. Some hunters of vermin, however, do prefer the flatter trajectory of the .177, feeling that the smaller pellet offers them the edge in accuracy. Against this, they must weigh the fact that the lighter pellet is a little more susceptible to being put off course by the wind in gusty weather conditions. At the end of the day, the decision must rest with the buyer.

I have hunted with many types of airgun in various calibres, and in my experience there is, generally, little difference between them in terms of effectiveness once their individual characteristics are fully understood. There are some situations, though, where the choice of calibre can make a difference. Grey squirrels are a pest in many woodland areas, and are fair game for the hunter. Ideally, with any vermin, a head shot is best, but I can remember, as a teenager, hunting these animals with a fairly powerful .177 air rifle, and my ability was perhaps a little less than ideal. I discovered that although a head shot would produce an instant, humane kill, an upper body shot was often ineffective, with follow up shots being necessary to despatch the animal. This I found disturbing, and close examination showed that the pellets had often passed right through the animals' bodies without imparting sufficient shock for an instant kill. Subsequent experience has shown that this situation is less likely to occur when .22 calibre is used (see Chapter 5 for further details).

## ❏ Types of Airgun

Most of the makes of gun mentioned so far have one thing in common: they are spring powered. It is true to say that some are break-barrel types and others under-lever or side-lever, but the power comes from air which is forced out under pressure when a powerful steel spring gives up its energy as the trigger is released.

There are other types of airgun, however. Pump-up guns store a charge of air, which is then released at the pull of the trigger, either in a single rush or in a controlled series of bursts, giving several successive shots for each charge. The idea is not new, and has been utilised with varying degrees of success in many vintage airguns, although the use of modern materials for seals and valves has greatly improved the reliability and predictability of these weapons.

Many of the best known airguns in this group are made in the United States, but match shooters will know that Germany also produces high quality competition airguns using this system, and Spain and Japan have made examples of this type of gun,

## Airgun Shooting

*Selecting a gun can be tricky with so many to choose from.*

too.

The American Crosman, Sheridan and Daisy come most readily to mind in the field of pump-ups. Quality is very much related to price, with the cheaper ones being very poor indeed, and the more expensive examples often underrated. This is perhaps due to the dubious reputation some of the early American imports to Britain had as regards reliability. These guns were considered, rather undeservedly, as being all-

## Choosing an Airgun

*A vast array of seemingly similar weapons is available and it is easy to make a wrong choice.*

powerful, and were credited with highly fanciful velocity figures in the days before instruments such as chronoscopes were available. Consequently, ambitious owners would pump them up well beyond recommended limits, destroying valves and seals in the process. Today, the law requires that safety release valves be built in so that legal muzzle energy figures cannot be exceeded, although high power versions are available for firearm certificate holders.

Advantages of pump-ups, or 'pneumatics' as they are sometimes called (strangely, since all airguns are technically pneumatics or 'air powered' weapons), are that there is no recoil on

## Airgun Shooting

*Select a gun which is suitable for the use to which it is to be put, and if possible try it out before buying.*

discharge, and accuracy tends to be very good. These guns can also be left in a charged state for long periods without the worry of a spring to deteriorate – a great advantage when hunting.

On the negative side, pump-ups, depending upon type, often need up to half a dozen or more pumps to charge them, and this can be both noisy, if you are hunting, and exhausting if you are plinking. Styling is often limited by the need to have a large pump lever incorporated into the design.

Apart from spring and pump airguns, there have come onto the market recently the results of some innovative ideas which have much to commend them. These ideas have been developed with the hunter in mind, but the guns concerned have also given a good account of themselves in field target competitions, and a great future is assured, provided that long-term reliability proves to be good. The indications are that, after a few

*Select a gun which suits your build.*

initial 'hiccups', this will indeed be so.

The Theoben Sirocco utilises an inert gas to power the piston. The gas is permanently sealed in and is compressed on the cocking stroke. Like the pneumatics, the Sirocco may be left cocked and ready to fire for long periods without damage. This is useful when hunting, but is generally not a good idea from the safety viewpoint. The Sirocco is recoilless and well made, and is consistent from shot to shot.

Saxby Palmer, whose pioneering work is now continued by Brocock, successfully introduced the concept of the air cartridge. Development was influenced by the military market in recognition of the fact that a relatively inexpensive airgun, using a cartridge which could be made compatible with military calibres, could have attractions as a training medium.

The air cartridge holds both the pellet and the charge of air

## Airgun Shooting

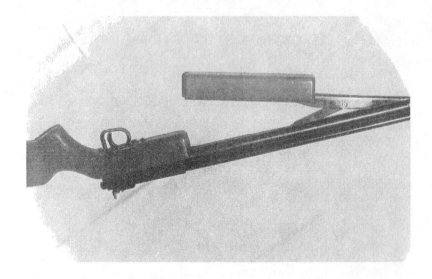

A pump-up 'pneumatic' rifle, showing the pump in the open position.
This is a Sharp Innova, of Japanese manufacture.

which propels it. Advantages include a lack of movement on discharge, and the ability to load a number of cartridges for repeating fire, subject to the design of the gun.

On the negative side, recharging and loading the cartridges can be time-consuming, making these airguns unsuited to plinking, although multi-loading facilities are available which improve matters considerably in this respect.

Although expensive, air cartridge weapons currently available are very well made and worthy of consideration.

Imported $CO_2$ or gas powered weapons are occasionally offered for sale, but it should be understood that these guns require a firearm certificate in Britain, as do any air rifles which exceed the limit of 12 foot pounds muzzle energy (6 foot pounds in the case of air pistols). Gas operated weapons do, in fact, need a firearm certificate regardless of muzzle energy.

## Choosing an Airgun

Incidentally, the Theoben Sirocco already mentioned does not fall into this category because the gas used is retained. It simply powers the piston, which then pushes the air before it and pushes the pellet out. So, it is still technically an air, rather than a gas, gun.

Pre-charged airguns have gained in popularity despite a relatively high initial cost and fairly high running costs. These accept a charge of air from a compression cylinder, usually of the type used by divers, and the stored charge enables a considerable number of shots to be taken before power falls off to the detriment of accuracy.

The best of these weapons have succeeded in minimising the effect of power fall-off and are very well made indeed.

In common with pump-up airguns and those using pre-charged cartridges, pre-charged airguns suffer little or no movement on discharge, making them very useful for certain types of competitive shooting: field target shooting in particular.

The cost of buying such a weapon and the need to buy recharged cylinders are important considerations, but many enthusiasts consider that the considerable advantages outweigh the disadvantages.

'Soft' airguns are a relatively recent introduction. These are comparatively low-powered airguns, often styled upon classic firearms designs, which fire small plastic balls reminiscent of the BB shots which are still used in some repeating airguns.

Soft airguns are intended for plinking – casual shooting at indoor or garden targets, and they have a repeating facility. Some fire several shots together, giving an effect rather like a shotgun, and hold many hundreds of plastic balls.

The low power of these airguns can lead to their being treated as toys, but it should be understood that they are quite capable of inflicting injury and should be used with the same care accorded to any other gun.

Paintball guns are usually pre-charged weapons firing a large calibre biodegradable ball which is full of water-soluble red or orange marker paint. They are used in war games such as 'Skirmish', where opposing teams in protective gear compete to achieve military objectives, 'shooting' each other in the process. Head shots are definitely no-go.

The use of these guns is tremendous fun, but falls outside the

*Airgun Shooting*

scope of this book.

## Chapter 3

# Somewhere to Shoot

It will be apparent that there is little point in buying an airgun if you have nowhere suitable to use it, yet surprisingly many people do make this mistake, probably because they have a vague notion that 'any open space will do', having perhaps seen others out shooting. We have noted, however, that it is easy to break the law in this respect.

## ❑ Plinking

In practice, most newcomers to the sport start in their own gardens or yards, and spend many happy hours firing away at improvised targets. Casual shooting at random or improvised

*Plinking good fun!*
*Airgun shooting is a growing sport attracting all age groups.*

*Airgun Shooting*

targets is known as 'plinking', an American term which probably derived from the sound of a pellet striking a tin can, a much-used target with plinkers. Plinking is immensely popular and undemanding. It does not require the self-discipline of formal competitive target shooting, or the patient dedication of the hunter; in short, plinking is great fun. That is not to say that other forms of airgun shooting are not fun, just that plinking tends to be a little more relaxing.

## ❏ Setting up a Backstop

There are just a few basic points to bear in mind when plinking in your own, or a friend's, garden. An adequate backstop or pellet trap should be set up behind the target area to catch and absorb the energy of spent pellets, and to prevent them from straying outside the boundaries of the garden. A backstop can be made from any appropriate materials, so long as it is large enough to catch the occasional 'flyer' (erratic shot). A few thicknesses of old carpet, or a large cardboard box stuffed tightly with newspapers laid flat, one on top of the other, will do an adequate job. Other good backstops are thick steel sheets, and even brick walls; but be warned, if a pellet strikes a hard surface at any angle other than a right angle, the resulting ricochet can cause a lot of damage. If you use steel or brick as a backstop, make sure you shoot at right angles to the target area. Avoid using bricks as a backstop if they present a facetted surface, as this, too, will deflect pellets.

The only time a backstop can be dispensed with is when you are hunting or shooting in large open spaces, but in these instances it is essential to ensure that nobody, and nothing breakable, is within range. Remember, a high powered air rifle is capable of ejecting its pellet at around 800 feet per second in .177 calibre, or around 600 feet per second in .22 calibre. A pellet can remain in flight for a couple of hundred yards or more and still retain enough of its energy at the end of its flight to cause damage or injury. Never underestimate the power of an airgun.

## ❏ Types of Target

Part of the fun of shooting is in devising new and interesting types of target. Card targets are enjoyable enough, and enable you to gauge your performance by making specific score comparisons over a period of time. Targets which offer some sort of reaction when hit give a little more colour to the sport. Tin cans have always been popular, and make a satisfying noise when hit, but lower powered guns will cause pellets to bounce off steel cans, so be careful. This problem is unlikely to occur with soft drink or beer cans as these are now made from aluminium, which offers little resistance to even a low powered pellet.

Handymen may like to make a mobile type of target, such as one with hanging figures which jump when hit or one with resettable pegs. Steel is the best material to use, and should not be less than about 16 SWG thickness otherwise it will quickly distort and collect plenty of dents if your airgun is reasonably powerful. Again, be careful to avoid ricochets.

It can be very enjoyable to shoot with other enthusiasts, and the competitive edge which this gives your shooting can greatly improve your standards of accuracy. Simple games are easy enough to devise, using all sorts of target, and scoring on a simple points system is usually appropriate, with the highest scorer being the winner.

## ❑ Local Clubs

The ideal vehicle for competitive shooting is, of course, your local airgun club, which is next on the list of places where you can use an airgun legally. In recent years, many new clubs have sprung up all over Britain, offering friendly advice and practical help to new shooters. Ask your local airgun dealer for details of clubs in your own particular area, or study one of the excellent magazines which cater specifically for airgun users, as these frequently contain addresses of such clubs. Failing that, the police will often be able to advise you.

Clubs for airgun users vary widely in the emphasis they place on the various aspects of shooting with airguns. Some clubs are geared for indoor card target shooting, and may be keen on serious competitive shooting at national or even international level. Such clubs will usually insist on .177 calibre only, as this is the recognised calibre for formal target shooting.

Field target shooting clubs have become very popular, giving members the chance to fire all types of airgun in .177, .22, or even .20 calibre on an outdoor range at varying distances. This type of club offers excellent training for anyone who intends to control vermin using an air weapon, and advice is always on hand for the newcomer. In my view, nobody should attempt to shoot at vermin unless they have first proved their consistent competence on a practice range – shooting at various distances, and under differing conditions and stances. Field target clubs offer just such experience.

Almost any type of air rifle or pistol is acceptable at most field target clubs, and you will have the opportunity of seeing and perhaps even trying out many varied weapons, including those which you would otherwise never have had a chance to try.

## ❏ Starting your own Club

Assuming that there is no airgun club within practical distance from your home, you may like to think about the possibility of starting your own club. This is not a venture to be undertaken lightly. It could involve a good deal of work, but you may be fulfilling a need amongst many other enthusiasts in your area. The first step in forming any sort of club is to find other people with similar interests and enthusiasm, either by 'putting the word around' or by advertising in shop windows, or in the local newspaper. If you are ambitious enough, you may like to consider an article in one of the national airgun magazines, too.

The most difficult aspect of forming a new airgun club is finding a suitable venue. Great powers of tact and diplomacy will be required to persuade the appropriate individuals that you are a serious-minded enthusiast.

Pubs may have a room available for hire, provided you can convince the landlord that there is no chance whatever of ricochets, or damage to the room. Make sure that you take out appropriate insurance cover first though, and ensure that all your members are conversant with basic safety rules.

It is possible to make folding screens using plywood, with layers of thick carpeting and felt to absorb spent pellets, and these screens can be left on the premises ready to erect on club night. Pubs are popular venues in many parts of the country.

## Somewhere to Shoot

Army and territorial units sometimes have small indoor ranges which you may be able to rent on evenings when they are not in use, by contacting the local C.O. Quite a few shops are now installing ranges for the use of prospective customers; if you are on good terms with the owners, it may be possible to use their ranges when they are not required, provided the security of their premises is not jeopardised. Large garages or basement cellars can also be used as airgun ranges. There is no real shortage of potential sites for an indoor club.

Outdoor shooting for many, however, is what airgun shooting is all about, and if you can find an old quarry and can track down the owners you will have the ideal, safe venue for your field target shooting club.

Whatever premises you seek for your club, be prepared to pay for your shooting, and if you can obtain the security of a lease, so much the better. As a matter of courtesy, let the local police know about your club, and never be afraid to ask the advice of the police firearms officer regarding any legal aspects about which you may wish to know.

Your club, be it indoor or outdoor, will need to be organised along formal lines, with proper accounts for members to see on request. There should be a management committee to decide

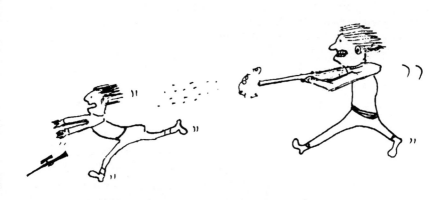

*Always seek permission to shoot on private land.*

upon rules and general policy, to establish the standards of the club, and to oversee safety aspects. A chairperson should be nominated to control and direct periodic meetings, a secretary to keep the minutes of those meetings, and a treasurer to handle finances. These are the basic requirements for any such organisation.

## ❏ Vermin Control

You may prefer, however, to shoot alone, or in the company of just one or two friends. Perhaps, after plenty of practice in the garden, you see yourself as a hunter, trudging home after sunset, your air rifle over one shoulder and a plump, tasty rabbit over the other. Vermin control is a subject which is explored in detail in my book 'The Airgun Shooting Handbook' published by Peter Andrew Publishing, but where to find a suitable hunting area is what we now have to consider.

It is fair to say that mainland Britain has a vast number of rabbits, wood pigeons, crows and rats, all of which are classed as vermin, and all of which are legitimate quarry for the airgun hunter. It is also fair to say that somebody else usually owns the land on which these creatures can be found, so your efforts must be directed:

(a) at finding the chosen quarry, and
(b) at gaining permission to shoot.

Should you turn up at a farm in scruffy jeans or camouflage gear, with your air rifle slung across your shoulder like some Mexican bandit, then ask permission to shoot, it is most unlikely you will be successful. Put yourself in the landowner's shoes, and imagine a stranger confronting you with a request to wander through your land, past your cows and sheep, shooting at vermin with a powerful air rifle, and ask yourself what your answer would be!

The best way of securing a shoot, as this type of hunting venue is termed, is to ask someone who knows you quite well if you can shoot over his or her land. If you do not know any landowners yourself, arrange for some friends or colleagues to introduce you to a landowner of their acquaintance.

Failing this, there is nothing to stop you knocking on doors and asking permission, but do dress respectably, and be polite, even if permission to shoot is refused. Do not expect something for nothing; always offer to pay for your shooting, or to help around the farm. This may well swing the chances in your favour. Above all, make it clear by your attitude and actions that you are a responsible sort of person who will respect and observe the Countryside Code, and who will have due regard to safety and concern for other people's property. Experience has shown that shooting rights are more likely to be obtained by an individual request rather than by two or three airgunners approaching a landowner together.

Point out the positive aspects of your sport. Arable farms are often plagued by wood pigeons, particularly during the winter months when food is scarce, and an offer to thin these out, occasionally, may be well received by a busy farmer who has little time to hunt vermin himself. Rabbits, as well as pigeons, can be a very worrying threat to crops which are particularly vulnerable at certain stages of their development, and a determined and responsible attempt to reduce the rabbit population may again be welcomed.

Apart from farmers, there are a number of organisations, such as local authorities, government departments and private firms, which often have overgrown tracts of land, surplus to immediate requirements. These areas of land may be unfenced, and unofficially used by unauthorised shooters already. In these cases, a written request should be made, preferably typewritten and stating your specific requirements and exact intentions regarding the use of the land, i.e. frequency of intended use, type of quarry, and any payment which you are prepared to offer. Your letter should be addressed to the head of the organisation concerned and, if possible, you should also enclose a copy of a plan detailing the area over which you hope to be allowed to shoot.

If you meet with success in your efforts, the acceptance letter should be photocopied, and the copy carried around with you when you shoot, as evidence of your right to be there. The owners might well welcome the chance of having an unofficial warden on their land, and may request that you report trespassers. Any conditions laid down by the organisation must be strictly observed, and avoid leaving litter or disturbing wild creatures which are not officially classed as vermin.

Finally, if all else fails, you can, like many readers of the national airgun magazines, advertise your requirements in the

## Airgun Shooting

hope that some farmer will take pity on you and offer you a shoot. In fact, a small number of enterprising farmers already advertise their own facilities to hunters. If you have the money and are prepared to travel, you are more or less assured of a shoot somewhere in the country.

# Chapter 4

# Using the Gun

## ❏ Zeroing the Sights

Having bought your gun, it will be necessary to zero the sights, regardless of whether you intend to use the standard, or 'open', sights or a telescopic sight.

The idea of zeroing is simply to ensure that the sights of the gun are correctly lined up. This will ensure that the gun is capable of hitting the target accurately at the distance at which you intend to shoot.

Start by ensuring that the gun is in good condition, with no loose screws or bolts. Ensure there is no excessive play in pivot pins, and check that the sights are securely fitted and cannot vibrate loose. It is particularly important when using a telescopic sight ('scope), which may work loose if not securely fixed with good quality mounts. In the event of severe 'scope creep, if an arrestor block is not available, a little thin paper smeared with impact adhesive will often provide a cure, as long as the mounts are tightened onto the paper first, rather than directly to the gun.

The method of adjustment may be by setscrews, ramp, or a knurled wheel or similar arrangement, and there will be adjustment for elevation (up and down) and windage (side to side). Adjustment is carried out on the rearsight only, with the foresight almost always being fixed, though on some guns a degree of elevation may be provided on the foresight.

Set up card targets, using a suitable backstop, at the distance at which you expect to do much of your shooting, then take time to establish a comfortable firing point. Bales of hay or cushions are best to enable you to achieve a rock-steady, rested firing position. Do *not* lean the gun on the rest when firing, but hold it in a comfortable firing position and use the rest simply to prevent movement as you fire. Keep pellets handy so that you do not need to alter your position while firing.

*Airgun Shooting*

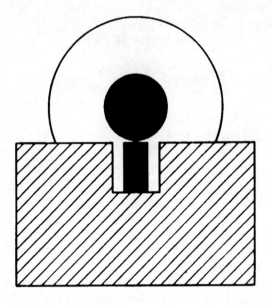

*The foresight blade should be centred in the blade of the rearsight and flush with the top of it*

**Figure 4.1 Sighting**

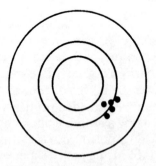

*Move rearsight to left and elevate it slightly to move group onto centre of target*

**Figure 4.2 Zeroing**

# Using the Gun

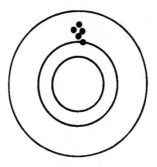

*Lower rearsight little by little to move group onto centre of target*

**Figure 4.3 Zeroing**

## ❏ Open sights

When sighting with open sights, the forsight blade or bead should be central in the rearsight V or aperture, depending which is fitted. The top of the foresight should appear flush with the top of the rearsight notch, or central if an aperture rearsight is fitted. Obviously, if a 'scope is fitted, it is a simple matter of lining up cross hairs, or hairs and post, or whatever set up the 'scope uses.

With open sights it is a good idea to keep a small area of white target above the sights, lining up just below the bull instead of spot on. This makes for better consistency, in that the black sights do not show up well against the black centre of the target.

The trigger should be gently squeezed, avoiding any tendency to pull or jerk. Each shot should be aimed at *exactly* the same spot, regardless of where the pellets go, and four or five shots should be fired at the target before any move is made to go and look at the result, assuming that the pellets are at least hitting the card of course.

If your shooting has been steady and the gun is in good condition, you should find that all the shots you have fired are clustered in a fairly tight group somewhere on the target card. If they happen to be in the bull, there is no need to read on, since the gun is shooting spot on and obviously suits your own

*Airgun Shooting*

*Telescopic sight adjustment.*
*The one at the top is for elevation, and the other for lateral adjustment.*

eyesight and method of shooting. You can congratulate yourself on your prowess, too.

However, if, as is more likely, the holes are all in one corner or other of the target, then some adjustment will be necessary.

Ignore any 'fliers', and simply take note of the trend of the pattern of pellet holes. To raise the pattern of hits, assuming that they are falling low, simply raise the rearsight a little at a time, firing a further four or five shots each time until the pattern is level with the centre of the target. Obviously if the shots are going high it will be necessary to lower the rearsight.

To move the point of impact to the left, adjust the rearsight to the left, and vice-versa if the shots need to fall further to the right.

To sum up then, move the point of impact *up* by *raising* the rearsight. Move the point of impact to one side by moving the rearsight in the direction you want the shots to go.

The important point with zeroing is not to be in too much of a hurry but to allow your shooting to be as consistent as possible, otherwise you could find yourself doing the job all over again as your technique improves. Try to obtain as much target practice as possible, but avoid shooting when you are tired, as your performance will fall off noticeably.

## ❏ Common Faults

As with most sports, bad habits picked up early on can take a long time to eliminate, but having said that, be sure that what you are trying to correct really is a bad habit and not just an individual way of shooting – the two are not necessarily the same, and many experts in various sports have their own particular technique which works well for them.

The classic fault among shooters, including many who should know better, is *trigger snatching*. The results of this fault, and it really is a fault, are inconsistency from shot to shot, and a predominance of 'fliers' (erratic shots) is inevitable. Snatching is caused by impatience and giving insufficient thought to the shot. If your gun has an adjustable trigger, it will be possible to reduce the weight at which the trigger lets off, and this will help to reduce the tendency to snatch. Don't overdo it though, or the airgun could become unstable and fire unexpectedly, with possible dangerous consequences. A competent dealer will be happy to carry out the job for you, if you prefer.

The trigger should be gently squeezed, with a smooth, steady movement. There should be no attempt to anticipate the point at which the gun actually fires, because that is indicative of the second commonest shooting fault, flinching.

## ❏ Flinching

Flinching is common among newcomers to firearm or shotgun shooting. Nervousness or anticipation of the explosion of the shot, albeit a small one, when the gun fires causes a jerky motion as the trigger is released.

Airguns are, of course, much less noisy than firearms, yet flinching is nevertheless still common among airgun shooters. Fortunately, this fault is usually eliminated as the shooter gains familiarity and confidence with the weapon.

A good marksman develops a rhythm to his shooting, so that even his breathing does not influence the quality of his shots. He knows that the wavering of the gun when it is being lined up

## Airgun Shooting

*Some different targets.*
*These are mounted on a thick steel backing plate to absorb the energy of the pellets.*

on the target is actually quite normal, and can never be totally eliminated, only controlled. Beginners are often alarmed by the fact that the gun barrel seems to have a mind of its own, and trembles uncontrollably, but in fact the art is in accepting this to a degree, and then knowing at which point to release the trigger.

Allow your shooting to be governed by a fixed series of movements. Cock and load the gun, release the safety catch if one is fitted, raise the gun to a point above the target, then lower it to just below the centre of the target. Finally, edge the sights up a fraction until the bullseye is lined up with just a narrow band of white below it, if you are using a conventional target card.

By the time you reach the point at which the shot is released, you should have already begun to squeeze the trigger very gently. Constant practice and familiarity with the gun will enable you to coincide the release of the trigger with the lining up of the sights on the appropriate point on the target, without snatching or otherwise spoiling the shot.

## ❏ Holding the Sights

A common fault among airgun users, particularly beginners, is to attempt to hold the sights on target for too long. If the shot is not fired fairly soon after coming on target, the weight of the gun will cause it to waver, as will the natural effect of breathing, and accuracy will be lost. Arrange your preliminary actions so that you are gently exhaling as the sights are lined up for the shot, but if you are unable to take the shot reasonably quickly, lower the gun for a moment or two and then start again, when the breathing rhythm has steadied.

The quality of shooting will obviously be impaired if attempts are made to shoot immediately after an arduous walk or climb. The body needs time to recover, to settle heartbeat, breathing and tired muscles, and these factors are vital to consider when hunting, because it is tempting to take a shot at a rabbit, for instance, which you have laboriously stalked for the last hour, as soon as you are at a point which affords a clear, in-range shot. You owe it to the rabbit, if not to yourself, to prepare yourself properly for the shot, particularly as you are likely to be contending with other problems, such as thistles, sharp rocks, and possibly pouring rain.

I have already stressed the need for safety at all times when using an airgun. Always be aware of your surroundings, watching out in particular for small children, who have little understanding of danger. Remember, the responsibility rests with the one using the gun, regardless of how stupid or inconsiderate the actions of others may prove to be.

## ❏ Pistols

Most newcomers to airguns start with an air rifle, whereas in my own case I started with an air pistol. Perhaps for this reason I have always had a particular interest in pistols, and have quite a large collection of them. I feel, too, that they offer a greater challenge, being more difficult to shoot well than a rifle, and anyone persevering with an air pistol will gain considerable satisfaction when they develop the necessary skill.

## Airgun Shooting

*The pistol should be treated as an extension of the hand.*

The basic techniques already described also apply in large measure to air pistols as well as to rifles. The only real difference is that the pistol is not so well supported as the rifle, and the task is to work at providing steady support for the shooting arm.

Constant shooting, especially with a fairly heavy pistol, will eventually strengthen the arm and wrist muscles, giving improved control. Matchmen shoot with one hand only, keeping the other hand out of the way by putting it in a pocket, or hooking the thumb into the waistband of the trousers. If you intend doing any match shooting your technique will need to be similar to this.

Those whose lives depend on the fast, accurate use of pistols employ the two-handed technique, with the non-shooting hand supporting the hand holding the pistol and, in practice, this can give a steady aim and a correspondingly high standard of accuracy.

A pistol should be treated as an extension of the hand, and sighting can be visualised as the action of pointing a finger. In fact, many successful pistol marksmen shoot almost instinctively, rather than depending solely upon the sights, and there are many stories about some marksmen removing the sights of their pistols completely and still turning in scores which would embarrass most of us.

If you are using open sights against a dark target you may find that they do not stand out too well. This problem can be overcome by putting a small amount of typewriter correction fluid over the upper edges of the sights. The material rubs off reasonably easily if you feel the need to remove it at a later date.

# Chapter 5

# Understanding Ballistics

Ballistics is a rather frightening word, which conjures up a picture of serious faced, white coated scientists employed by the Ministry of Defence, huddling over complicated testing equipment, or perhaps police pathologists studying a bullet taken from the body of a murder victim in an effort to establish which gun, or type of gun, fired the fatal shot.

In fact, ballistics is simply the term used to describe the study of the behaviour of any type of projectile in flight, be it a stone, bullet, or even a guided missile. From the airgunner's point of view it is the study of how pellets behave once they have been fired. It may sound unnecessarily technical, but it is, nevertheless, important for the shooter to have at least a basic understanding of what an airgun pellet is doing on its flight from the barrel to the target. Such a knowledge will enable him to gauge the likely behaviour of the pellet under a given set of circumstances.

## ❏ Smooth and Rifled Barrels

Most modern air weapons, except the very cheapest examples, have rifled barrels rather than smooth bores. That is to say, the interior of the barrel is machined to leave shallow grooves in a gradual spiral pattern for the whole length of the barrel. These grooves grip the pellet as it is propelled through the barrel by the charge of air behind it, and the pellet emerges from the muzzle rotating on its axis. Gunsmiths and the military discovered many years ago that imparting such a spin to a projectile causes it to travel with greater accuracy and consistency on its path to the target. Rifling also enabled streamlined projectiles to be used, which are less likely to be affected by wind resistance than spherical missiles, and are thus more efficient over a longer range. Fired from a smooth barrel, a bullet-shaped projectile will gradually tumble in flight, allowing wind

# Understanding Ballistics

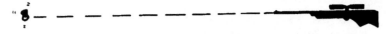

*Smooth bored barrel – the pellet tumbles*

*Rifled barrel – gyroscopic action keeps pellet straight*

**Figure 5.1 Effect of smooth and rifled barrels**

forces to act upon a greater surface area and deflect the projectile from its intended path.

The principles of rifling were discovered as early as the sixteenth century, but were not really developed until much later. It was not until breech loading came into being that the full potential of rifled barrels could be realised. With the old muzzle loaders, loading was difficult and tedious, and likely to be dangerous if a rifled barrel was fitted. In such a case the projectile had to be forced past the rifling grooves before it was seated and ready for firing. Consequently, the traditional smooth-bored muskets remained popular until breech loading overcame the problems associated with rifling.

The effect of rifling on the flight of the pellet may be clearly seen by comparing pellets fired at a hard steel surface, first from an airgun with a rifled barrel, and then from a smooth bored airgun. At close range, the front of the pellet will be dented in each case, to a greater or lesser degree, depending upon the velocity of the guns used. Shoot from a greater distance away from the target, though, and then compare pellets. The rifled barrel weapon will continue to produce pellets which are dented at the front, but the pellets fired by the smooth-bore gun will be dented on the front, sides or back; in fact anywhere.

The reason for the difference is that rifling induces a gyroscopic action in the pellet, which makes it resistant to the forces of the air acting upon it. A pellet from a smooth-bore gun, however, gradually turns in the air as it is propelled along by its charge of air. As it turns the air catches at the uneven surfaces, unless it is a perfect sphere, and flips it in several directions. This accounts for the relative inaccuracy of smooth-bored guns. Obviously, the higher the velocity of the gun, the greater the eventual margin of error is likely to be when the pellet eventually strikes its target. The higher velocity will have a correspondingly greater effect on the pellet as it begins to tumble.

Manufacturers are able to get away with installing smooth-bore barrels in lower priced airguns because, owing to the lower power of the cheaper guns and the correspondingly shorter effective range, the reduced accuracy is less apparent than in a more powerful gun. Smoothbores can be simple brass-lined tubes, whereas a steel rifled barrel must be carefully machined using special, equipment. A rifled barrel is, therefore, more expensive to produce. As a youngster I shot with a smooth-bored Diana air rifle, and was able to shoot with consistent accuracy, but only at ranges of up to 7 or 8 metres. This range is perhaps acceptable for a youngster, but not for an experienced shooter.

## ❏ Trajectory of the Pellet

Gravity is another force which acts upon projectiles in flight, as well as air turbulence and general wind resistance. The effects of all these forces can be best illustrated by throwing stones. A large, heavy stone requires a considerable amount of energy to propel it. Its passage can be seen as a fairly steep curve – the stone travels in an arc as it leaves your hand. To overcome the weight of the stone and the effect of gravity, it is necessary for you to propel it at a very steep angle, and it returns to the ground at a similar angle. Throw it into a high wind and it is unlikely to travel as far as if you had thrown it *with* the wind.

Launch a lighter stone and you will discover that it can be thrown at a shallower angle than the large stone to reach the same distance for a given expenditure of energy. It then also returns to the ground at a similar shallow angle, or trajectory. Throw the lighter stone into the wind and it *may* be less affected than its larger brother because it has less surface area on which the air can act. On the other hand, its lighter weight makes it easier for the wind to act upon it in flight, influencing the flight path which it takes through the air.

*Understanding Ballistics*

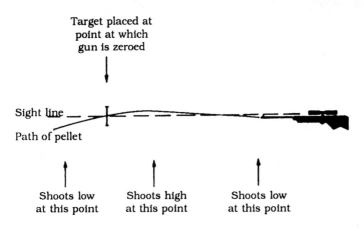

**Figure 5.2 Trajectory of pellet**

Relating this example to the question of which calibre to use - does the lighter, smaller pellet travel faster and, therefore, further for a given amount of energy than the larger pellet? Will it not also travel in flatter trajectory, instead of curving steeply as it travels? Will this fact make it a more accurate and generally better calibre to use?

The answers, unfortunately, are not entirely straightforward. The trajectory curve – the flight of a small, light pellet like a .177 through the air on its way to the target – will be shallow, more of a straight line than the pronounced curve of the trajectory of a heavier, larger pellet like a .22 or .25, and consequently the allowance needed on elevation (up and down adjustment) for long range shots is less for the smaller, lighter pellet. A gun zeroed at 20 metres may well still be almost spot on at 10 or even 20 metres more, whereas the use of a larger calibre will necessitate adjusting the point of aim by several centimetres for the same range variation. In a sense it may be said that the .177 is more accurate than a larger calibre.

Some would argue that because a small calibre pellet can travel very fast, needing relatively little energy to propel it, it may be less prone to being knocked off line by side winds than a heavier pellet. Proponents of the heavier calibres might correspondingly suggest that the weight of the slower moving heavier pellet makes it less of a pushover for any passing

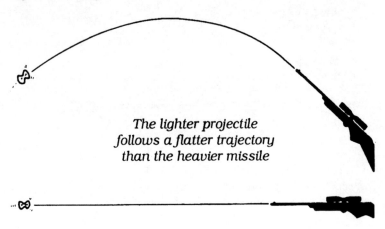

**Figure 5.3 Comparison between light and heavy missile trajectories**

breeze. There is actually relatively little solid reliable scientific evidence available regarding airgun ballistics. The much lower velocities than those attained by firearms mean that data obtained from firearm testing is not necessarily applicable to airguns. Experience has in fact shown this to be the case, though obviously some aspects will be the same. Perhaps the reason for a shortage of firm data relating to airgun ballistics is that there are many factors involved, each capable of affecting one or more of the others. The effects of rifling have already been mentioned. Small variations in individual rifle barrels, even on the same make and model gun, can make a difference, as can variations in pellet type, effects of rifling on the pellet, damage to the pellet itself, etc.

My own experience, which has not really been very scientific, is that the lighter .177 calibre is inclined to be more affected by sidewinds than the .22, but this is the result of casual observation using a relatively limited number of weapons. The results may well be very different if a wider range of airguns is used, and tests carried out at various distances, using different makes of airgun, firing different configurations and weights of pellet: remember that pellets can vary in weight depending upon type. Accuracy and performance can be influenced by the considerable weight variation between individual pellets of identical type and calibre within the same batch. You will see that the task of carrying out objective, meaningful testing is not as straightforward as it might at first appear.

## ❑ Pellet/Airgun Combination

It might be assumed that .177 is more desirable as a calibre than .22 by virtue of the fact that the pellet travels faster, and is, therefore, more likely to be effective in penetrating the target, than the larger calibre. This assumption only tells a part of the story though, because the speed of the pellet is just one of several factors involved in the effectiveness of that pellet as a vermin killer. The weight of the pellet is another factor, as we have seen by comparing the performance of thrown stones of different sizes. The actual type, or configuration of the pellet is also important.

With regard to the effectiveness of a pellet/airgun combination when shooting live vermin – and it is very relevant to match a particular airgun to a pellet which has been proved to suit it – the vital point is to give consideration to what exactly it is that kills the animal. This may seem an irrelevant statement at first; after all, it is the pellet which kills the animal. That is true, but does the animal die of loss of blood, damage to vital organs, shock, fright, or a combination of these things?

When a pellet leaves the barrel of an airgun, it carries a certain 'charge' of energy. This charge of energy is related to the velocity at which the pellet is propelled by the charge of air behind it, and also to the weight of the pellet itself. The energy is imparted from energy stored in the coiled spring (assuming a spring air weapon is being used) and released when the trigger is pulled. As the pellet travels on the path from the muzzle of the gun, this initial 'muzzle energy' (which as we have already seen is limited to 12 foot pounds for an air rifle, and 6 foot pounds for a pistol) gradually reduces as the pellet speeds towards the target. Wind resistance, gravity, air turbulence, pellet weight and shape all have an effect upon the trajectory. By the time the pellet reaches the target, for example, a rabbit, the energy 'stored' in the pellet may be down to, say, 6 foot pounds from an initial muzzle energy of 11 or 12 foot pounds, depending upon range and other factors. As the pellet strikes the rabbit, some or all

of that residual energy is given up into the body of the animal.
  Let us assume that a high velocity .177 or even .22 air rifle is fired at a rabbit at, for instance, 20 metres. The hunter is a beginner who does not feel confident enough in his ability to take a head shot, so he aims at the upper body of the rabbit, which presents a much larger, easier target. The pellet strikes the chest area of the animal, passing through skin first, then flesh, and finally, missing the bones of the rib cage, the pellet speeds on, giving up part of its energy as it does so, through resistance of the body tissues. The pellet misses the heart and other vital organs although there is localised tissue damage, and then passes out of the other side of the chest of the rabbit to expend the remainder of its energy in a rocky bank or other obstacle behind the animal.
  The rabbit leaps high into the air as it is hit, then runs, apparently unharmed, for thirty or forty metres before disappearing into cover. The hunter thinks he has missed the rabbit, as it does not appear to be damaged in any way. He may leave the area to search for another, and the same thing may well happen again. If he should study the ground where the animal was hit, he may discover droplets of blood but more likely there will be no indications of a successful hit at all; any bleeding usually tends to be internal, in view of the small size of an airgun pellet. The hunter may be no wiser even after careful scrutiny of the area where the rabbit was shot. The rabbit may possibly survive if the wound is fairly clean, but is more likely to die a slow, lingering death over a period of hours, or even days.
  The above scenario is not fanciful fiction, but is based upon actual experience and observation. Consider now another example.
  A hunter with a slightly lower powered air rifle, in .22 calibre, takes a shot at a rabbit from 20 metres, and hits it in the chest. The pellet strikes the bones of the rib cage and breaks one of the ribs, fragments of which tear through the lung area, causing severe internal bleeding and impairing the animal's breathing. The energy of the pellet has been fairly well expended by striking the bone, and it continues to travel more slowly, and in a different direction, because it has been deflected by the bone. It finally comes to rest inside the chest cavity, just below the heart; all its energy has been expended inside the animal.

When the pellet hits the bone, fragments (being of soft lead) fly off the main part of the pellet and tear through soft tissue before their energy, too, is used up. The nervous system of the animal suffers a severe shock as a result of the energy transfer from the pellet. This, coupled with sudden, severe loss of blood from vital areas torn by fragments of pellet and bone, causes a quick death.

Often, with this last type of hit, the rabbit may leap into the air and start to run. It may even reach cover, but dies very quickly. I have read of game animals in Africa being shot and then running for a quarter of a mile before collapsing in death. Perhaps nervous energy propels the muscles even as death occurs. However, whatever the reason, one point is clear – always go for a head shot when shooting live animals, or risk losing the animal and, worse, causing it to suffer.

Apart from the obvious value of head shots when shooting vermin, there are a number of lessons to be learned from the two examples detailed above. It will be clear that a larger pellet has more chance of hitting something important as it strikes the target. The higher the velocity, the better the chance of a pellet passing right through the animal without giving up all of its energy inside the animal's body. This point is likely to be academic anyway if the pellet, regardless of velocity, strikes a vital organ, since death is then more or less assured. A larger pellet entering the body of an animal must have a greater effect on the nervous system than a smaller pellet, and will impart a correspondingly greater degree of shock, and so improve the chances of a quicker kill.

It is, for instance, quite possible to kill a small animal or bird by hitting it with a projectile which does not even penetrate the body. Marbles or ball bearings fired from catapults come to mind here, and the shock of being struck by a large, albeit quite slow moving projectile is often sufficient to kill quickly, without any penetration of the body, and often without even severe tissue or bone damage.

The reason is that the large missile represents a substantial amount of energy. On impact, this energy is given up into the body of the target animal, imparting a massive, potentially lethal shock to the nervous system. Even without other damage, shock can and does kill. It is also one of the greatest killers of people, and is one of the reasons why accident victims are

*Airgun Shooting*

encouraged by the emergency services to go to hospital for a check up even if they have no obvious injury.

Evidence of the effects of shock have been known to the military and to firearm users for many years. Certain modern weapons in current use fire a small bullet at a very high velocity. The shape of the bullet is such that it tumbles on impact, causing a severe wound and associated shock, and can kill, even when a non-vital area is hit. The old wild west cowboys knew that the big .45 calibre bullet travelled relatively slowly, and had a short range when fired from a handgun, but it was a sure man-killer. High velocity small calibres could not be relied upon to do the same job.

## ❏ Pellet Construction

Pellet construction has a part to play in successful, clean kills, too. Some types of pellet are solid and heavy for their size. Their weight makes them formidable when they impact, expending their energy, and they are inclined to tumble when they hit, creating a severe wound channel and imparting a high level of shock. They stay in one piece as they strike and do not fragment, and any damage is limited to that done by the main pellet itself.

Some non-lead pellets do not flatten on impact, and consequently penetrate better. This can be an advantage, as the further the pellet travels, the more likely it is to hit something important. On the other hand, it may travel right through without giving up enough of its energy to kill, though this type does tend to tumble on impact, and then stop quite quickly.

Almost as a contradiction to our tests with the stones, some light alloy pellets are so light that they lose momentum too quickly to be effective at long ranges. A degree of compromise is obviously called for when selecting a suitable pellet.

Soft lead pellets have advantages and disadvantages. If you like to eat the rabbits you shoot, the presence of lead fragments in the meat is unlikely to help your digestion, and can cause lead poisoning. From the point of view of the hunter though, the traditional lead diabolo shaped pellets do quite an efficient job.

Diabolo pellets travel through the air very well and are fairly light for their size, giving a straighter trajectory and consequently good accuracy. They deform very easily when they

## Understanding Ballistics

strike bone, and a misshapen pellet causes more tissue damage than a perfectly formed one. Even if they do not become deformed they often tumble on impact, giving a similar effect. Soft lead pellets also fly apart if the velocity is high enough and the bone sufficiently hard, and this can do considerable damage. In practice, small animals and birds have fairly fragile bones which offer no real resistance but they do their part in absorbing the energy from the pellet well enough and a firm shock to the nervous system of the animal is ensured.

The diabolo pellet has certainly stood the test of time, and still outperforms just about every other pellet configuration in its various guises. The shape of the diabolo is not perfect from the aerodynamic point of view, but it has two points of contact with the rifling (more in some newer designs) which reduces friction compared with pellets or bullets that have continuous multiple contact with the rifling. The cutaway design of the diabolo reduces weight, increasing velocity, size for size.

*Some pellet configurations (left to right):*
*Pointed, Roundheaded, Prometheus, Sabot, and Wadcutter*

Perhaps the best design, albeit probably one which is difficult to manufacture, would be an aerodynamic bullet shape, with a 'boat' tail to reduce drag. It would have two shallow driving bands to grip the rifling, one at the front, the other at the rear. These would be soft, so that they would flatten by the time the pellet left the barrel to avoid upsetting the aerodynamics of the projectile more than absolutely necessary. Lastly, the pellet would be hollow, so that on impact it would deform considerably, causing greater tissue damage and consequently shock to the quarry. Being hollow, the velocity would be good, and all the energy would be transferred to the target by the pellet's deformation when it hits the target. Perhaps some form of weakness lines could be built into the pellet without affecting aerodynamic principles. Such lines could allow the pellet to mushroom more effectively on impact. The principle of hollow point bullets, which mushroom on impact, causing a massive shock wound, is already established in the firearms field. Although hollow point airgun pellets are available, there is scant evidence to indicate that they expand any more than a standard pellet at a given velocity. There is nothing wrong with the principle, but since soft, hollow lead pellets spread on impact anyway, it is hard to see any benefit from using hollow pointed pellets unless, as I have suggested, pellets could be made with built-in weakness lines, without adversely affecting their performance in flight. Whereas a loss of velocity of, say, a hundred feet per second in a firearm would not be noticed, a similar loss in a projectile from an airgun could not be tolerated.

It will be seen, then, that the matter of ballistics holds as many questions as answers. Surely, though, this is part of the great attraction of airgun shooting, as we seek constantly after improvements, learning from our disappointments and building on our successes.

# Chapter 6

# Competitive Airgun Shooting

Having shot your air rifle or pistol on your own for some time you may well become curious to know how well your shooting compares with that of other airgun enthusiasts. Many people start to take a step towards competitive shooting by inviting a friend around for a plinking session. It is inevitable that you will compare scores, finding out who is able to knock over the most tin cans, hit the bullseye on a card target the most times, or turn in the highest score over half a dozen target cards.

If your performance is good and you consistently shoot high scores, then it is only natural you will want to compete against a much wider field. The answer is to join your local club and make a note of all competitions which are coming up. There are open competitions advertised from time to time, and you may prefer to shoot in one of these before deciding whether to join a club. An open competition is simply a shooting match in which the entries are not restricted to club members only, as many matches inevitably are.

## ❑ Open Competitions

To compete in an open competition just read the published rules, or send for full details, enclosing a stamped addressed envelope for the reply. Usually competitors can turn up on the day and shoot, but sometimes it is necessary to obtain an entrance form, pay a fee in advance, and shoot at a specified time.

If field target shooting is of interest to you, there is a separate chapter devoted specifically to this branch of the sport in my book 'The Airgun Shooting Handbook', published by Peter Andrew. This chapter covers general aspects of competitive shooting, and is intended to let you know what is available to those who have an interest in competitive shooting.

## ❑ Bell Target Shooting

Should you happen to live in the Midlands, you have probably already heard of bell target shooting. Sometimes referred to as the 'pints and pellets' or 'pellets and pints' sport, bell target shooting is a well established sport which has been in existence for more than a hundred years. It reached a peak during the years between the First and Second World Wars. It suffered something of a decline after the Second World War but has regained popularity in recent years, together with the resurgence of interest in airguns generally.

Bell target shooting has traditionally been associated with pubs and working men's clubs, where the sport has always been taken very seriously, with leagues being established alongside the local darts or snooker league, and clubs travelling back and forth to compete against one another. There is a certain appeal in shooting at a target that makes a noise (hence the popularity of the ubiquitous tin can), and bell target shooting appeals audibly as well as socially.

There is no doubt that this is indeed a social sport, and many clubs have traditionally vied with one another to attract the best marksmen. A good bell target shooter is not necessarily the best marksman though. In the boisterous atmosphere of a pub or club, with comments being bandied back and forth, glasses rattling, people shouting, and smoke wafting across the target area, it can be very difficult to concentrate fully upon shooting well. As a consequence, the successful bell target shooter is probably someone who shoots well, but can also handle the rowdy atmosphere and remain unaffected.

Very much a team sport, bell target shooting is for those who enjoy a lively social aspect to their sport. Round or pointed pellets are used at 6 yards in two series of 10 shots in 15 minutes, with two sighting shots before each series and a 20-minute interval.

## ❑ Running Boar Shooting

A type of shooting known as running boar shooting was introduced at the 1972 Olympic Games in Munich as a small-bore rifle shooting event. It was not long before the sport was adapted to suit airguns.

The original running boar shoots were 50 metre events for firearms but the adapted version utilises .177 calibre 'scoped air rifles, shooting at a range of 10 metres. The target is a picture of a European wild boar and has concentric target circles marked on it. It is motor driven to cross a two metre opening in five seconds, or two and a half seconds. The targets come in pairs, one facing the left and the other facing to the right. This type of shooting is not unlike snap shooting in that there is a limited amount of time allowed (or available) for the actual shot.

Some clubs buy the running boar ranges ready built, and there are a number of different designs available at various costs. Some enterprising clubs build their own running boar systems and, provided they satisfy the required standard of operation, these serve perfectly well, and allow many shooters to sample running boar shooting who would not otherwise have the opportunity to do so. This type of shooting is reminiscent of fairground shooting of ducks and ping pong balls, so it tends to capture people's imaginations. It has even been featured on television, which is usually the hallmark of a fairly wide acceptance of a sport.

## ❑ 10 metre and 6 yard Target Shooting

Established indoor target shooting, apart from the bell target shooting already mentioned, is available as two distinct disciplines. These are 10 metre and 6 yard target shooting. You will find clubs offering both types of shooting, but some clubs specialise, so if you have any particular preference it is worth checking beforehand.

You will be required to use only .177 calibre for either discipline. A recoilless rifle (or pistol) will eventually prove to be a necessity if you are really serious about competitive target shooting, since only these guns have the consistency to produce regular high scores. That is not to say that other types of airgun are not effective, merely that we are talking in terms of millimetre accuracy, and any slight edge which a better gun may give you needs to be seized upon, if you are to make an impact upon the competitive target scene. For this reason, it

## Airgun Shooting

may be wise not to buy a gun immediately upon joining a club, as a club gun is often available, or you may be able to borrow one. Naturally, a recoilless airgun of top quality is not cheap, and it is, therefore, important to be absolutely sure that target shooting of this type is definitely for you before laying out large sums of money on equipment.

10 metre target shooting is a little more demanding than 6 yard target shooting because of the greater range involved, though it may seem to be a relatively insignificant difference at first glance. What this means in practice is that scores tend, on average, to be a little lower for 10 metre target work than 6 yard, since any aiming errors that exist are magnified over the greater distance. Even more care is, therefore, needed at this range, with particular attention being paid to breathing, rhythm, firing stance, and other factors.

In 10 metre shooting, scoring is by a method known as inward gauging. The higher score counts if the pellet has broken a line on the target card. The card itself carries one or five individual targets of black on white, and a full match course at 10 metres is of unlimited sighting shots, with 40 or 60 shots to be counted. A time limit is imposed, and the course of shots must be fitted into one and a half hours for Ladies and Juniors, and two and a quarter hours for Men. Local variations exist.

6 yard target shooting follows similar lines to the 10 metre discipline, except that the target cards differ and take account of the shorter range.

Match rifles use dioptre sights, with interchangeable foresight ring and variable rear aperture. Pistols use open sights.

## ❏ Postal Competitions

Finally, if you are not too keen on travelling all over the country to shoot competitively, postal competitions are popular. Many clubs participate in these, and they give airgun users the opportunity of competing in nationally organised events without stepping outside their own club, except perhaps to compete in the finals, once the preliminary results are made known.

Authenticated and witnessed target cards are sent off to the adjudicating body which has organised the postal competition. The results are then collated and competitors graded according to results, so that they are able to compete with others of similar aptitude.

Organisers of postal competitions usually insist that target cards are sent in 'as shot', without having been gauged first. Other rules relevant to this type of contest are supplied to the individual on receipt of the entry form, together with any fee which may be payable.

## ❏ Trigger Pressure

When it comes to target shooting on a competitive basis, there are rules and regulations relating to the guns and other equipment to which you need to adhere, and full details of these are provided by the organisers of each competition and should be studied in depth. If you are a pistol enthusiast and intend competing at either 6 yards or 10 metres, you will need to ensure that the weight at which the trigger of your pistol releases is not less than 500 grams. The better quality pistols have finely adjustable triggers, and a light trigger helps to reduce excessive movement of the pistol when firing. This is an advantage, provided it is not below the specified minimum. A very light trigger can be dangerous and, in addition, if you have been practising using an ultra light trigger setting then you will have become accustomed to shooting at that setting. Should you enter a competition and have the pistol checked, you will be asked to adjust the trigger to the specified weight. You may then be likely to find that your scores suffer because you are unused to the new trigger weight. Other checks include maximum weight – 5 kg for rifles, 1.5 kg for pistols – and dimensions.

The trigger let off pressure can be gauged by the use of an accurate spring balance with the appropriate metric calibration. The test should be carried out with great care to ensure safety. Cheap pistols are not generally provided with an adjustable trigger and the standard weight is likely to be well above the 500 grams limit, unless the pistol has been modified by a specialist or by the owner.

I have, for the most part, deliberately avoided recommending particular makes and models of airgun for a specific purpose, as the market is constantly changing, and new developments may supersede even tried and tested favourites in quite a short time, rendering any information that I may offer out of date very quickly. For this reason, I recommend that the newcomer makes an effort to study the equipment which others are using, and to listen to their views, especially the views of those who are clearly successful at their sport. Do not simply buy the gun everyone else is using at a particular club. It may not necessarily be the best gun for you, so be prepared to ask questions in a bid to find out why one particular gun is so popular.

## ❏ Points to Note in Achieving Accuracy

There are, in fact, relatively few top flight target air rifles which have the features necessary for consistent pinpoint accuracy, i.e. placing successive shots through the same hole at 6 yards. Such a rifle needs to be recoilless, superbly balanced, and matched carefully to the individual who is to use it. For this reason you will find that competitions are dominated by just a few specialist target weapons. Before laying out your hard-earned money to buy one, be absolutely sure that you settle for a gun which suits you in all respects, and is naturally capable of the sort of accuracy which I have described.

When plinking, pinpoint accuracy is rather less important than in competitive target shooting, and faults which develop in shooting technique can be overlooked to a degree. This is not the case in competitive target shooting, however. Successful marksmen look for every possibility of improving their shooting to give them an edge to their performance, and perhaps clinch a match for them. Plinking can actually be harmful rather than beneficial to good target shooting if bad habits are allowed to continue unchecked. It is obviously necessary to recognise a fault for what it is, before it can be corrected.

* **Stance**

This is important. If the body is unbalanced or uncomfortable it will not be possible to achieve the best scores consistently. If the stance is wrong it becomes all too easy to hold the gun at various angles in relation to the target without being aware of it. Stance can be studied in detailed books on target shooting, but like many other aspects of airgun shooting, a good stance owes much to common sense. If the feet are placed far enough apart to ensure stability, and if the body is placed in such a way that it is comfortable and so that the gun comes up on aim

## Competitive Airgun Shooting

smoothly and without wavering, then the main purpose of a good stance will have been achieved.

* **Fitness**

One point which is not always fully understood, even by experienced shooters sometimes, is that it is necessary to be physically fit in order to shoot well at competitive target shooting. Your blood needs to be well supplied with oxygen to keep you alert and prevent disturbances in the rhythm of your breathing, which will need to be monitored carefully as you shoot. You should be fit enough to hold up the rifle without swaying or wavering unduly. Although well balanced, a target air rifle is likely to weigh in excess of 10 pounds. This is a considerable weight when you bear in mind that you will be holding it in the aiming position to take a shot on numerous occasions during the course of a competition.

Holding the gun on aim for too long, or even doing too much shooting at one time, can seriously affect accuracy, and will

*It is necessary to be physically fit in order to shoot well in competition.*

*Airgun Shooting*

also show up any deficiencies in the shooter's personal fitness. With a target air rifle weighing in at around 10 pounds or so, any weaknesses in wrist, arm, shoulder, or other upper body muscles will quickly make themselves known.

* **Breathing**

Perhaps a good argument, if any were needed, in favour of competitive target shooting could be that it helps to keep you fit. A big beer belly and a persistent smoker's cough are not likely to boost you to the higher echelons of the competitive airgun marksmen.

Good breathing rhythm is important. Many beginners make the mistake of consciously holding their breath too long before they fire. This upsets the body's natural rhythm, altering heartbeat, causing deeper breaths to be taken to compensate, and depleting the body of oxygen temporarily. The shots should be taken during the natural break between breathing out and breathing in, and this break can be extended a little with

*Good breathing rhythm is important.*

practice. Exhaling should be gentle and measured as the gun is brought up to the aiming point, and the shot can then be taken when the lungs are empty.

The faults of snatching and flinching have already been described in chapter 4, and are common faults which need eliminating early on. Snatching is not always easy to correct, especially if the shooter is trying to avoid holding the gun on target for too long and is taking the shot before he is really ready.

* **Sighting**

When sighting pistols, the top of the foresight should be level with the top of the rearsight notch, and should be central in the rearsight. The sights should be horizontal and not placed at a slight angle; a good stance will help to achieve this. To be sure that the sights are aligned and setup as they should be, the aiming eye should be focused upon the sights rather than upon the target. As a result, the target itself will appear a little indistinct, but do not worry, that is perfectly correct; the sights are the important thing upon which to concentrate.

* **Hold**

A comfortable and steady hold of the rifle or pistol is also important and needs to be right so that movement is minimised and the sights readily aligned. It is possible to learn some aspects of hold by studying specialist shooting books but, as a general guide, if the gun feels comfortable and comes on aim quickly with the minimum of adjustment and, provided none of the faults mentioned exhibit themselves, it can usually be assumed that all is well.

Avoid falling into the trap of becoming so familiar with a particular gun that you overlook any shortcomings. Be critical in self analysis and of your equipment. Take nothing for granted and you stand a good chance of turning in scores comparable with the best.

* **Choice of pellets**

When a target shooter reaches the stage of ironing out all the little imperfections in his equipment and in his own method of using it, he may possibly begin to be over concerned about the pellets he is using. The flat-headed 'wadcutter' type of pellet is generally used in indoor competitive target work as it gives a clean, non-ragged hole in the target card, making accurate scoring easier. Although a little less aerodynamically efficient than, say, pointed pellets, the wadcutters offer excellent accuracy at the ranges involved. At short range, velocity variations are rather academic, provided they occur only when the type of pellet used is changed, and not from shot to shot.

There is little point in spending a substantial amount of money on a top recoilless target air rifle, then using just any old pellets which happen to be on hand. The pellets you choose to use must be proven to be effective in your gun, and that, as far

*It is a mistake to use any old pellets for competitive target shooting. Pellets should be individually selected and be compatible with the gun used.*

as target work is concerned, means that they must be very accurate. Should you be hunting, obviously you would look for pellets which are able to offer an acceptable muzzle energy when used in your gun, but for target work at the relatively short ranges involved, accuracy is all.

It is impossible to recommend any particular make or model of pellet, since the requirements of each gun, sometimes even of the same model, are different. The bores of German air rifles, for instance, while nominally the same as their British counterparts are actually fractionally different, so a broad guide is to use German pellets in German airguns, and British pellets in British airguns. This is something of an over-simplification, of course, and there are plenty of exceptions, but be sure of what they are before adopting a particular pellet.

The major problem with lead pellets is that, being of soft metal, they deform very easily, and it always surprises me that pellets supplied in tins, as most are now, are not more damaged than they usually turn out to be, especially when you consider how tightly packed they are. The possibility of using a deformed pellet, which obviously is going to be less accurate than a perfectly formed pellet, can be reduced in a number of ways.

Some manufacturers supply their pellets in dispensers which hold each individual pellet separately from its neighbours. This ensures that any deformity can only occur after the pellet has been removed from the dispenser; so a basic cause of the occasional flier is eliminated at the outset. Pellets packed in this way are more expensive than mass-packed ammunition, but you may feel the additional cost is worthwhile. It is no good using one make of pellet for practice though, then changing to another for the big competition. Stick to one type of pellet for all your practising and competitive shooting.

Careful hand selection of pellets, eliminating those with imperfections, is another way of improving the odds in your favour. A magnifying lens will help you to study the pellets in some detail, but very careful handling is essential in order to avoid damaging any previously undamaged pellets. The skirts of diabolo pellets are particularly prone to damage, and while a certain amount of edge distortion to a pellet may be removed by the pressure of air and the passage of the pellet through the barrel, it is better to avoid risking inaccuracy by eliminating these pellets at the outset, especially if an important competition is involved.

° *Weight*

Some matchmen even go so far as to weigh each pellet to separate out those that fall outside a given range of weights. Obviously, the variations under consideration are extremely small, and normal weighing equipment is not sensitive enough to do the job. If you have access to a chemical balance you may feel the effort involved in weight selecting your pellets to be worthwhile.

Should you be reasonably adept, it is possible to make a small balance device which will help to select pellets that comply with the requirements. All that is needed is a simple 'see-saw' type balance, made of suitably light materials and critically balanced. Some small items (such as grains of sugar or salt, or tiny staples from a stapling machine) are needed which will counter balance the pellet, and which can be added or taken away until the pellet is balanced, having tested a suitably sized sample for accuracy. All pellets can be tested to ensure that they balance the scales. Those that do not can be rejected as being outside acceptable limits.

The actual weight of the pellets which you test in this way is not critical, since, being of a particular calibre (.177 for target work) and of the same make, the variation is going to be extremely small indeed, especially with the top makes of pellet which you are likely to be using. What is really important is that all the pellets are the same, regardless of whether 'the same' means relatively heavy or relatively light.

Having selected a batch of pellets for uniformity, they need to be carefully protected until they are ready for use. The few manufacturers who supply individually packed pellets have solved the problem for you, but pellets from tins need to be individually packed. There are a number of suitable materials which can be used for this purpose: foam rubber and expanded polystyrene come readily to mind. The material preferred by flower arrangers will also protect pellets. Known as 'Oasis', this material is a type of foam which can easily be cut out or bored to make holes to take the pellets. Unfortunately, it does tend to be a little messy.

° *Sizing*

Some shooters like to use a sizer on the pellets before loading them into the breech, and these devices help to ensure diametric consistency within a given batch of pellets. What they do is to even out any irregularities in the pellet surfaces which contact the barrel of the gun, and also ensure that each pellet is identical in diameter and thus conforms to the barrel of the gun when it is fired.

To some extent an airgun acts as its own pellet sizer. When an airgun is fired, a blast of air under considerable pressure hits the rear of the pellet which is seated in the breech. When a soft, hollow lead pellet is used, the air pressure behind it expands the skirt to some extent on firing, and so enables the pellet skirt to grip the rifling effectively, helping the pellet to conform to the barrel of the gun and eliminating leakage of air past the pellet, which would reduce the available power.

However, deformities in a pellet, particularly minor damage to the front driving band of the pellet, are unlikely to be much affected by the air pressure as the gun is fired, and as a result, any pellet with this type of damage, albeit slight, can prove to be a flier. A well made sizer can eliminate the fairly minor damage which may not be visible to the unaided eye. Hopefully you will have already weeded out any badly damaged pellets.

° *Seating device*

Some shooters like to use a pellet seating device. Some airguns have a tapered breech, so that a pellet which is being loaded simply enters and seats itself in the correct place. With other airguns, a pellet can be placed in the breech, yet without a firm push part of the skirt of the pellet may project over the face of the breech. When this situation arises in a break-barrel air rifle or pistol, the pellet skirt can be pinched and distorted as the gun is closed, and this is obviously disastrous for accuracy. Sometimes these pellets can fall out completely without being seen, resulting in a 'dry' shot, which can damage some airguns, often irreparably, depending upon design.

Any small stick, or a thin pen or pencil, maybe used to seat a pellet, but care must be used to prevent the slightest damage to the pellet in the process. The use of a device specially designed for the purpose will make sure that the pellet is inserted the same distance into the barrel each time, as this will ensure consistency.

I do not wish to give the impression that your shooting will not be successful unless you are heavily loaded with gadgets. That is certainly not the case; many successful airgunners use little more than their favourite airgun and a tin of pellets. It is as well to be aware of what accessories are available so that you can make up your own mind about their relative merits and demerits.

As discussed previously, the quality of your shooting will depend upon a number of contributory factors, including practice, preparation, personal skill, personal fitness, and quality of equipment.

This may seem a most formidable and an exceedingly complex challenge, but if the sport really does begin to feel like that to you then just take a metaphorical step back and look at it again – remember it is a very enjoyable sport.

# Chapter 7

# In Conclusion

The sport of airgun shooting is great fun, as all sports should be, yet it can present many different faces to its enthusiasts. It need not be expensive; a cheap secondhand airgun can provide many hours of casual enjoyment plinking in the garden, and for many this sums up all that they ask of the sport.

Others may enjoy the social aspects of joining a thriving club and shooting competitively and in company with others who share their enthusiasm for the sport.

Some may prefer a solitary approach to their shooting, perhaps combining it with a love of nature. Crawling through damp ditches in the countryside in an effort to outwit an alert rabbit or wood pigeon is not everyone's idea of fun, but for many of us, as with angling, it provides an opportunity to observe wildlife at first hand, and learn aspects of field craft.

Indeed, the control of vermin can actually become secondary to the sheer enjoyment of being able to commune with nature. As an angler I can also attest to the fact that, for the same reason, catching the fish is often almost incidental to spending a delightful day in quiet, unspoiled surroundings.

I hope that this book has provided you with a helpful insight into the sport of airgun shooting, and that you will have a desire to investigate the various forms that the sport may take. You will soon, like the rest of us, become 'bitten by the bug', and discover that you are a fully fledged enthusiast, boring your non-shooting friends with talk about the latest telescopic sights, field target scores and so on.

You may decide to stick with plinking in your garden. If so, you join many thousands of airgun users who do the same. Should you decide to specialise in Field Target Shooting or vermin control, or become interested in modifying or customising your airgun, you may like to take a look at the companion volume to this book entitled 'The Airgun Shooting Handbook', which expands upon these aspects of the sport and takes a look at what

*Airgun Shooting*

accessories are available.

## ❏ Airgun Users and the Public

It is no exaggeration to say that there is now, more than ever before, a greater awareness of conservation issues. There are great pressures for tighter controls upon gun users, including airgun enthusiasts, and high crime levels have focussed public attention on us.

Every airgun user has a personal responsibility, as an ambassador of the sport, to act within the law and to behave responsibly. Vermin control should not become an excuse to shoot upon public land or upon land where no permission to shoot has been given, or to shoot at protected species or domestic animals.

Safety must be the paramount consideration when shooting. Apart from the obvious tragedy of shooting accidents, each incident adds to the clamour for tighter controls on the use of guns.

I hope you have enjoyed reading this book, and that you will do your part to ensure that the public perception of our sport is a positive one.

Enjoy your shooting!

# Index

Agreements (for use of land) 28, 29
Air cartridge 19, 21
Airgun magazines 25, 26, 29
Air seal (see *Seals*)
Arrester block 31

Backstop 8, 24, 31
Ballistics 40, 50
BB shots 9, 21
Bell target shooting 52, 53

Calibre, choice of 14, 15, 43-48
Chronoscope 17
Clubs 25, 27, 65
Competitions (open) 51
$Co_2$ 20

Darts 9
Diopter sights (see *Sights, Aperture*)

Elevation 31
Entry fee 51

Field target shooting 26, 51, 65
Firearm certificate 17, 20

Gas guns (see $Co_2$)
Grading 62
Gun case/cover 6

Injury 1, 6
Insurance 26

Law 1-5

Mount 31
Muzzle energy/velocity 1, 2, 13, 20, 45, 61

Open competitions
 (see *competitions*)
Open sights (see *Sights*)

Pellets, choice of, 48, 59-62
Pellet holders 62
Pellet seating tools 63
Pistols 9, 11, 20, 37, 38, 54, 55, 59
Piston 21
Plinking 21, 23, 56
Pneumatics & pump-ups 15-18, 20
Port (see *Transfer port*)
Postal competitions 54
Power (see *Muzzle energy*)
Pre-charged weapons 21

Recoil 53, 56, 60
Running boar shooting 52, 53

Safety catch 9, 36
Seals 13, 17
Seat 63
Shooting rights (see *Agreements*)
Sights, Aperture 54
 Diopter (see *Sights, Aperture*)
 Open 33, 39, 54
 Telescopic 31, 33, 34
Sizers, sizing 63
Snap shooting 53
Soft airguns 21
Spring 15
Stance 56

Telescopic sights (see *Sights, Telescopic*)
Theoben system 19, 21
Trajectory 14, 42-44
Trrespass 4

Underlever 15

Valve 15

*Airgun Shooting*

Vermin 28, 45, 65, 66

Windage 31

Zeroing 31, 32, 34

# Other airgun books from Peter Andrew

## The Airgun Shooting Handbook
### by Les Herridge

This is the companion volume to Les Herridge's 'Airgun Shooting – An Introduction'. Contents include competitive airgun shooting; field target shooting; vermin control; mechanics; accessories; refinishing and customising.

## Vermin Control with the Air Rifle
### by Jim Tyler

This book is the first serious treatise on the subject from a universally recognised authority. Contents include the definition of vermin; selection of a suitable air rifle; sighting system and pellet; pellet trajectory; methods and tactics.

## Airgun Sport
### by Jim Tyler

Jim's second book delves deeply into all aspects of the sport of airgun shooting. An excellent read for both beginner and experienced airgun shooter.

## Airgun Field Target Shooting
### by Les Herridge and Ian Law

This authoritative book provides the reader with a comprehensive insight into this fast growing sport.